DO YOU REALLY WANT TO MEET A PTEROSAUR?

FABBR

AMICUS ILLUSTRATED and AMICUS INK
are published by Amicus
P.O. Box 1329, Mankato, MN 56002
www.amicuspublishing.us

EDITOR: Rebecca Glaser
DESIGNER: Kathleen Petelinsek

LIBRARY OF CONGRESS CATALOGING-IN-PUBLICATION DATA

Names: Pimentel, Annette Bay, author. | Fabbri, Daniele, 1978- illustrator.
Title: Do you really want to meet a pterosaur? / by Annette Bay Pimentel ; illustrated by Daniele Fabbri.
Other titles: Do you really want to meet...?
Description: Mankato, Minnesota : Amicus Illustrated/ Amicus Ink, [2018] | Series: Do you really want to meet a dinosaur? | Audience: K to grade 3. | Includes bibliographical references and index.
Identifiers: LCCN 2016057201 (print) | LCCN 2016058092 (ebook) | ISBN 9781681511139 (library binding) | ISBN 9781681521381 (pbk.) | ISBN 9781681512037 (ebook)
Subjects: LCSH: Pteranodon—Juvenile literature. | Pterosauria—Juvenile literature. | Dinosaurs.
Classification: LCC QE862.P7 P56 2018 (print) | LCC QE862. P7 (ebook) | DDC 567.918—dc23
LC record available at https://lccn.loc.gov/2016057201

Printed in China
HC 10 9 8 7 6 5 4 3 2 1
PB 10 9 8 7 6 5 4 3 2 1

ABOUT THE AUTHOR
Annette Bay Pimentel lives in Moscow, Idaho with her family. She doesn't have a time machine, so she researches the past at the library. She writes about what happened a long time ago in nonfiction picture books like Mountain Chef (2016, Charlesbridge). You can visit her online at www.annettebaypimentel.com.

ABOUT THE ILLUSTRATOR
Daniele Fabbri was born in Ravenna, Italy, in 1978. He graduated from Istituto Europeo di Design in Milan, Italy, and started his career as a cartoon animator, storyboarder, and background designer for animated series. He has worked as a freelance illustrator since 2003, collaborating with advertising agencies and international publishers, including many books for Amicus.

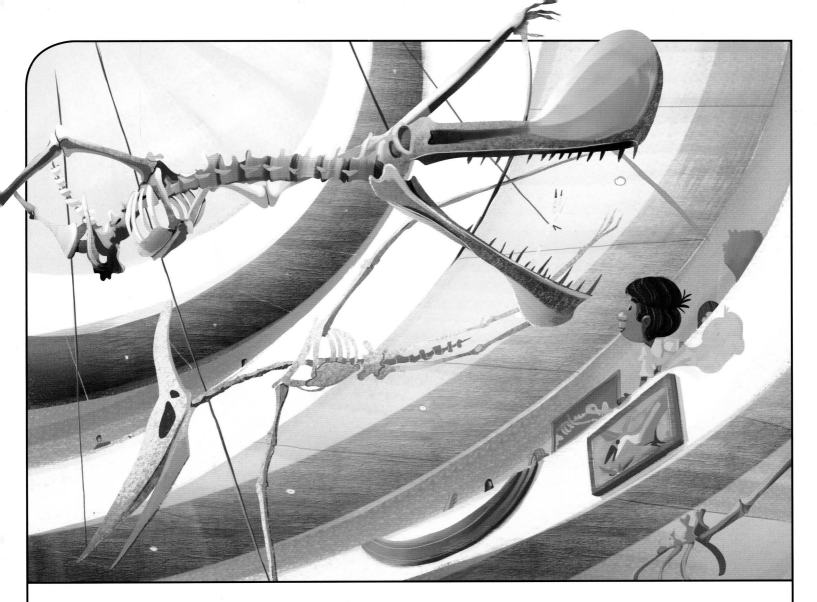

Is that a flying dinosaur? No. Dinosaurs couldn't fly. That is a flying reptile called a pterosaur. They lived all over the world during the time of dinosaurs. Would you like to meet one?

Which pterosaur would you like to meet? Some pterosaurs were about the size of robins. Others had a wingspan as big as a small airplane. Some nested on land near dinosaurs. Others flew long distances across oceans.

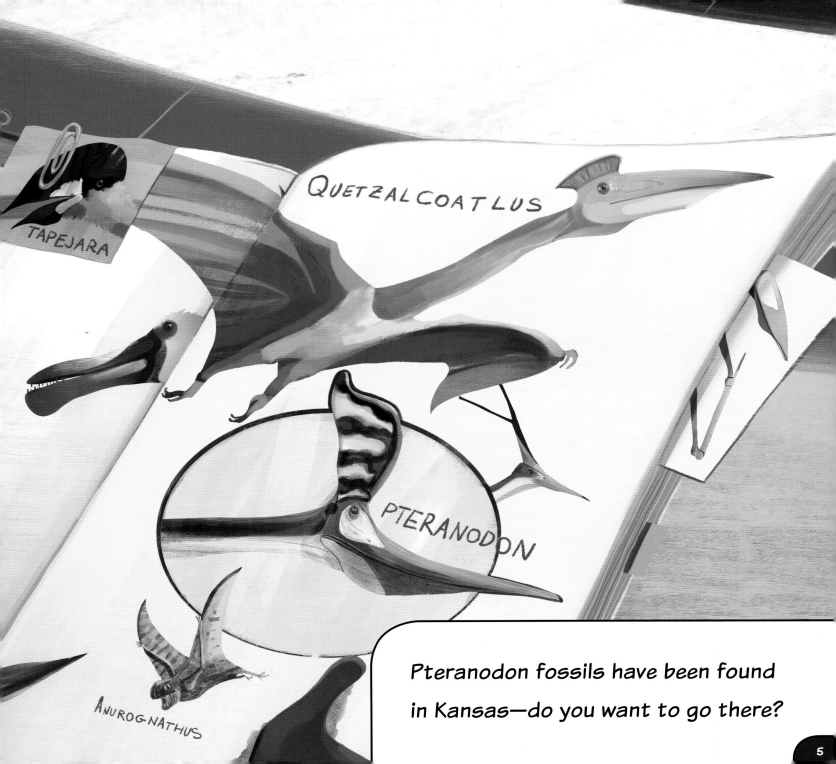

Pteranodon fossils have been found in Kansas—do you want to go there?

Okay. To see a Pteranodon, you'll need a time machine. Go back 80 million years to the Cretaceous Period, before pterosaurs and dinosaurs went extinct. Back then, Kansas was under a sea. Make sure your time machine can double as a boat.

Splash! You land near a flock of Pteranodons on the beach. With their wings folded, all you notice is their big heads and skinny legs. They're about as tall as you. Their bones are hollow. You weigh more than one of them!

A few Pteranodons are bigger. Those are the males. Their extra-large heads are longer than a baseball bat! They strut with their fancy crests to attract females.

Where is that female going? She's digging a hole for her soft, leathery eggs. They'll be safe underground.

But these other eggs are ready to hatch. Soon, the flapling will hop into the air. Even babies can fly!

A big one is taking off, too. It runs along the beach on four legs. Then it jumps and unfurls its wings. Now you see how big it is. The wings spread 20 feet (6 m) across. If Pteranodon were alive today, it wouldn't fit between football goalposts. Do you want to follow?

You won't be able to swim fast enough to keep up—take your boat. Pteranodon flies far from shore, often gliding on air currents. It rarely needs to flap its wings.

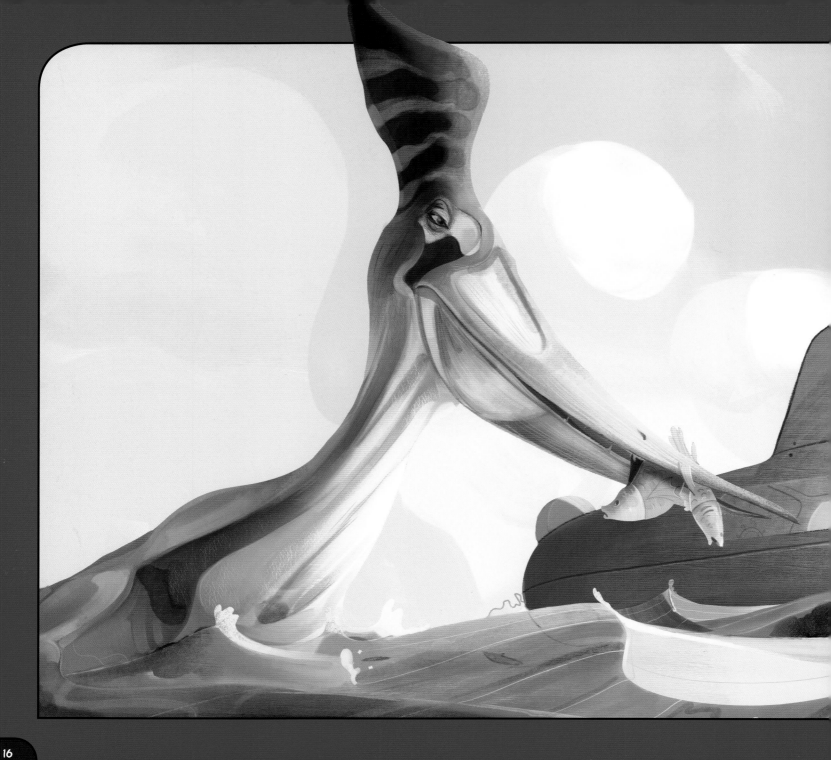

There is one in the water. What's in its long beak? Swim over to get a closer look. Pteranodons have huge beaks, but they don't have teeth. Luckily it's eating fish, not you!

Pteranodon seems restless. What's wrong? Something is circling below.

Dive down to check it out.

A shark! Pteranodon is in danger as long as it's in the water. So are you.
Swim back to your boat. Fast!

Pteranodon launches into the air. It can catch more fish later, after the shark has swum away. But your dinner is waiting back in your time. Better head home. Say goodbye to Pteranodon, the prehistoric winged wonder.

WHERE HAVE PTERANODON FOSSILS BEEN FOUND?

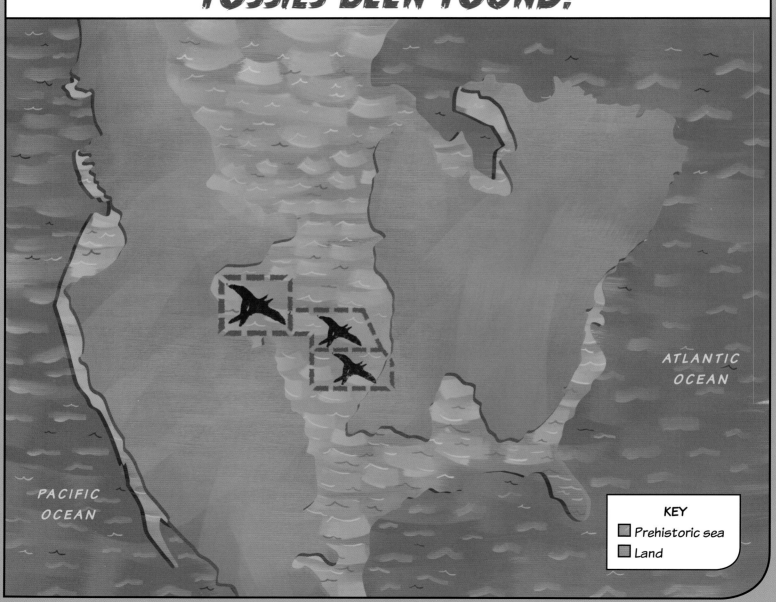

PACIFIC
OCEAN

ATLANTIC
OCEAN

KEY
Prehistoric sea
Land

GLOSSARY

air current—A natural movement of air.

crest—An outgrowth on the top of an animal's head.

Cretaceous Period—The time between 145.5 million and 65.5 million years ago. Dinosaurs lived during this time.

dinosaur—A large reptile that lived in prehistoric times and walked on land.

extinct—No longer found living anywhere in the world; known only from fossils.

flapling—A baby pterosaur.

pterosaur—A winged reptile that lived at the time of dinosaurs, and is closely related to dinosaurs, but is not a dinosaur.

wingspan—The distance between the end of one wing of an animal and the other.

AUTHOR'S NOTE

Too bad for us, time machines aren't real. But all of the details about pterosaurs in this book are based on research by scientists who study fossils. For example, scientists in Kansas have found pterosaur fossils 100 miles (160 km) from the shore of an ancient ocean. That means pterosaur's wings must have carried them far from land. They were real long-distance flyers! New fossil discoveries are made every year. Look up the books and websites below to learn more.

READ MORE

Alpert, Barbara. *Pterodactyl.* Mankato, Minn.: Amicus, 2014.

Lach, Will. *I Am NOT a Dinosaur!* New York: Sterling, 2016.

West, David. *Prehistoric Flying Reptiles.* New York: Windmill Books, 2016.

Zeiger, Jennifer. *Pterosaur.* Ann Arbor, Mich.: Cherry Lake, 2016.

WEBSITES

DINOSAURS: NATIONAL GEOGRAPHIC KIDS
http://kids.nationalgeographic.com/explore/nature/dinosaurs/
Compare sizes of dinosaurs, meet paleontologists, and more.

WHAT IS A PTEROSAUR?
http://www.amnh.org/exhibitions/pterosaurs-flight-in-the-age-of-dinosaurs/what-is-a-pterosaur/
This short video features scientists explaining facts about pterosaurs.

Every effort has been made to ensure that these websites are appropriate for children. However, because of the nature of the Internet, it is impossible to guarantee that these sites will remain active indefinitely or that their contents will not be altered.